ALL AROUND THE WORLD
CHILE

by Kristine Spanier, MLIS

pogo

Ideas for Parents and Teachers

Pogo Books let children practice reading informational text while introducing them to nonfiction features such as headings, labels, sidebars, maps, and diagrams, as well as a table of contents, glossary, and index.

Carefully leveled text with a strong photo match offers early fluent readers the support they need to succeed.

Before Reading

- "Walk" through the book and point out the various nonfiction features. Ask the student what purpose each feature serves.
- Look at the glossary together. Read and discuss the words.

Read the Book

- Have the child read the book independently.
- Invite him or her to list questions that arise from reading.

After Reading

- Discuss the child's questions. Talk about how he or she might find answers to those questions.
- Prompt the child to think more. Ask: Different climates are found throughout Chile. What is the climate like where you live? Does it change with the seasons?

Pogo Books are published by Jump!
5357 Penn Avenue South
Minneapolis, MN 55419
www.jumplibrary.com

Library of Congress Cataloging-in-Publication Data

Names: Spanier, Kristine, author.
Title: Chile / by Kristine Spanier.
Description: Minneapolis: Pogo Books, [2021]
Series: All around the world | Includes index.
Audience: Ages 7-10 | Audience: Grades 2-3
Identifiers: LCCN 2019036549 (print)
LCCN 2019036550 (ebook)
ISBN 9781645273264 (hardcover)
ISBN 9781645273271 (paperback)
ISBN 9781645273288 (ebook)
Subjects: LCSH: Chile—Juvenile literature.
Classification: LCC F3058.5 .S63 2021 (print)
LCC F3058.5 (ebook) | DDC 983—dc23
LC record available at https://lccn.loc.gov/2019036549
LC ebook record available at https://lccn.loc.gov/2019036550

Editor: Jenna Gleisner
Designer: Molly Ballanger

Photo Credits: tifonimages/iStock, cover, 12-13; John Elk III/Alamy, 1; Pixfiction/Shutterstock, 3; kavram/iStock, 4; galbiati/iStock, 5; takepicsforfun/Shutterstock, 6-7; Amy Nichole Harris/Shutterstock, 8-9; Cezary Wojtkowski/Shutterstock, 10; Arco Images GmbH/Alamy, 11; LarisaBlinova/iStock, 14; MARCELOKRELLING/iStock, 15; iFerol/Shutterstock, 16; vale_t/iStock, 16-17; imageBROKER/Alamy, 18-19; Hoberman Collection/SuperStock, 20-21; johan10/iStock, 23.

Printed in the United States of America at Corporate Graphics in North Mankato, Minnesota.

TABLE OF CONTENTS

CHAPTER 1

WELCOME TO CHILE!

Andes Mountains

Chile is the longest country on the planet! It is 2,653 miles (4,270 kilometers) long. The Andes Mountains run along the eastern border. This is the longest mountain range in the world!

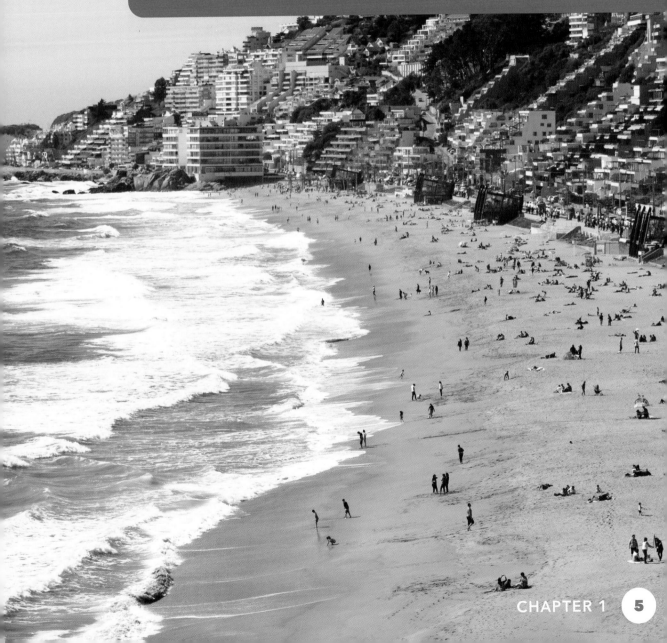

Chile is also the narrowest country. Some parts are only 40 miles (64 km) wide! It shares the southern tip of South America with Argentina.

Chile has three different **climates**. Atacama Desert is in the north. Some places here have never had rain! The center of the country is mild. It has rich farmland. The south has islands and **glaciers**. Cape Horn is the southernmost point of South America. It is only 400 miles (644 km) north of Antarctica!

glacier

TAKE A LOOK!

These are the three main climate **regions** of Chile. Why do you think the south is cold **tundra**?

CHILE●

ANTARCTICA

■ = desert
■ = mild
■ = tundra

● CAPE HORN

N
W ✛ E
S

Easter Island is a **territory**. It is 2,200 miles (3,541 km) from Chile. But it is part of the country. More than 800 stone statues are here!

WHAT DO YOU THINK?

How did Easter Island get its name? The first European visitors arrived on Easter! What if you could name an island? What would you name it? Why?

CHAPTER 2
LAND AND ANIMALS

Andean condor

Interesting animals live in Chile. The **national** bird is the Andean condor. It is the largest flying bird in the world!

The pudú is the world's smallest deer. It is only 15 inches (38 centimeters) tall.

copper
mine

The land is filled with **natural resources**. Copper is **mined** here. Chile is the world's largest **producer** of copper. It is an **export**. Grapes, apples, pears, and peaches are also important exports. So is seafood.

CHAPTER 3
LIFE IN CHILE

Do you like seafood? Sea urchins are a popular dish here. So are abalone. These are sea snails.

sea urchin

Maybe you would like to try empanadas. These are pastries. They are filled with meat or cheese. Yum!

empanada

Most of the people here live in cities. Valparaíso is one. It is an important **port** city. Ships carry goods in and out. Funicular cars make it easier to get to the top of this city.

WHAT DO YOU THINK?

Would you like to ride in a funicular car? How do you get around where you live? How is it similar or different?

◄ · · · · · funicular car

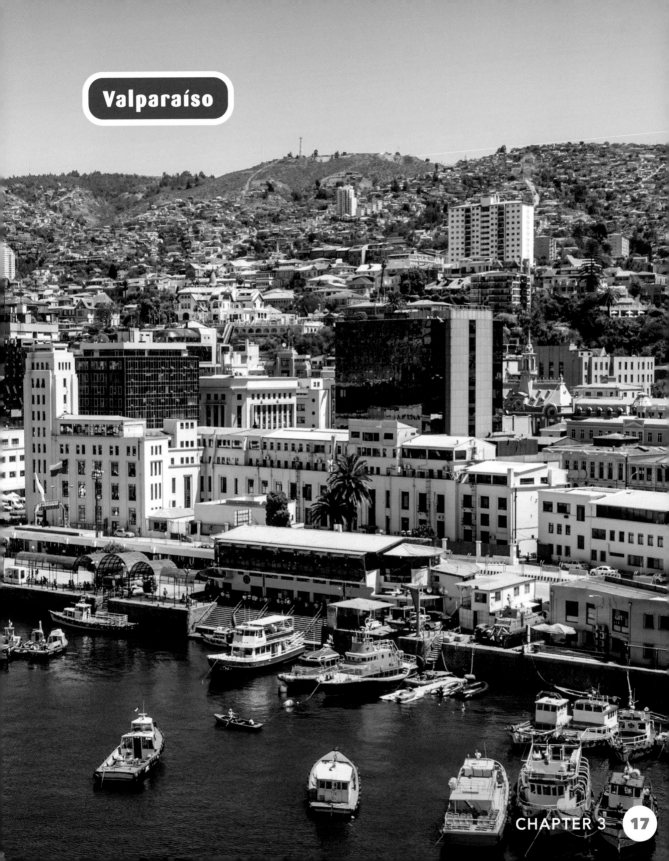

Valparaíso

uniform ·····▶

Children start school here when they are five years old. They must attend until they are 17. Many children go to public schools. Some go to private or religious schools. They wear uniforms every day.

DID YOU KNOW?

Santiago is the **capital**. The president is the head of the government. **Citizens** can vote when they are 18 years old.

VOTE

Chileans take part in many activities. Football, or soccer, is a national favorite. Many ski in the mountains. Others take part in rodeos. Chilean cowboys are called huasos. They wear bright clothing.

People stay busy in Chile! Would you like to visit?

QUICK FACTS & TOOLS

CHILE

Location: South America

Size: 291,933 square miles
(756,103 square kilometers)

Population: 17,925,262
(July 2018 estimate)

Capital: Santiago

Type of Government:
presidential republic

Languages: Spanish and English

Exports: copper, fruit,
fish products, paper and pulp

Currency: Chilean pesos

GLOSSARY

capital: A city where government leaders meet.

citizens: People who have full rights in a certain country, such as the right to work and the right to vote.

climates: The weather typical of certain places over a long period of time.

export: A product sold to different countries.

glaciers: Very large, slow-moving masses of ice.

mined: Dug up from the ground.

national: Of, having to do with, or shared by a whole nation.

natural resources: Materials produced by Earth that are necessary or useful to people.

port: A town with a harbor where ships can load and unload goods.

producer: One that grows agricultural products or manufactures crude materials into objects of use.

regions: General areas or specific districts or territories.

territory: Land under the control of a state, nation, or ruler.

tundra: A very cold area where there are no trees and the soil under the surface of the ground is always frozen.

Chile's currency

INDEX

TO LEARN MORE

Finding more information is as easy as 1, 2, 3.

❶ Go to www.factsurfer.com

❷ Enter "Chile" into the search box.

❸ Click the "Surf" button to see a list of websites.

FACT SURFER